YOU'RE PULLING MY LEG!

400 HUMAN-BODY SAYINGS FROM HEAD TO TOE

BY PAT STREET and ERIC BRACE

ILLUSTRATIONS BY ERIC BRACE

HOLIDAY HOUSE / NEW YORK

Dear Reader,

Do you have a green thumb? Wait—don't look at your hands to see! I meant "Are you good at growing plants?" "Green thumb" is a saying. Our English language is full of sayings—strange ones, wise ones and funny ones. In this book I've collected hundreds of colorful sayings about the human body.

Most sayings, like "green thumb," are idioms. Idioms don't make sense when you try to figure them out word by word. Instead, you have to know the meaning of the whole group of words. It's important to know common idioms so that you can understand what you read and hear.

Some sayings are similes, such as "Your feet are like ice." This simile compares feet to ice, and it means that your feet are very cold. Similes include the word "like" or the word "as."

Metaphors are also sayings that compare, only without using "like" or "as." One metaphor is "He wears his heart on his sleeve." This saying compares a heart to feelings. It means that he shows his feelings—everyone can see he's in love.

A proverb is a sentence that offers advice or wisdom. "Many hands make light work" means that if a lot of people help, the job will be easy.

Some sayings rhyme, like "Zip your lip." Some have alliteration—they repeat consonant sounds, like "half-hearted" and "lily-livered." Other sayings repeat vowel sounds, like "lamebrain."

Many sayings exaggerate, like "She's smiling from ear to ear." Of course, a smile can't really go from one ear to the other. The saying simply means that somebody's smile is very, very big. I hope you'll be smiling from ear to ear while you read this book.

Pat Street

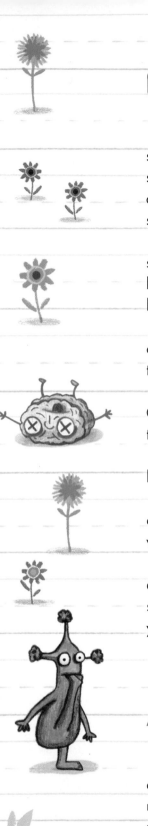

A NOTE FROM THE ILLUSTRATOR

After Pat submitted her manuscript it was my job to dream up the scenes, as well as writing the jokes and conversations. Hopefully, these additions not only make the phrases more fun, but also give them greater context and meaning. To use an idiom, this book was, "hands down" the most challenging project I've ever taken on. And to use another idiom, "it's with my whole heart that" I thank Mary Cash for her brilliant editing and Pat Street, Claire Counihan and everyone at Holiday House for their creativity and patience.

Eric Brace

Contents

It was eye-catching.
It was visually interesting.

I love this photo. It's so eye-catching.

an eye for an eye
The punishment should be as severe as the crime.

Keep an eye on him.
Make sure he stays out of trouble.

Officer, why would I take my sister's doll when I have this robot? And by the way, your eyeball is on my head.

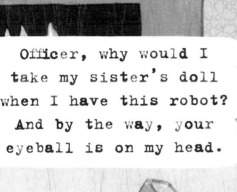

I've never even had a doll. All I have is an apple on a stick with bandages for eyes.

Beauty is in the eye of the beholder.
Beauty is a matter of opinion.

Don't fire until you see the whites of their eyes.
Wait until you're sure before taking action.

crying his eyes out
crying very hard

I pulled the wool over her eyes.
I fooled her.

an eyesore
something ugly to see

Good news, I found the doll!

That will raise eyebrows.
People will be shocked.

furrowed brow
forehead wrinkled in thought

Keep your eyes peeled.
Stay watchful and alert.

11

19

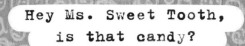

Hey Ms. Sweet Tooth, is that candy?

What candy? I don't see any candy! Mmmm...candy!

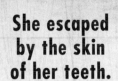

She escaped by the skin of her teeth.
She made a narrow escape.

She's lying through her teeth.
She is lying shamelessly.

I have a sweet tooth.
I love candy and desserts.

a law with teeth in it
an enforceable law

Keep your chin up!
Have courage!

a baby tooth
a temporary tooth which eventually falls out to make room for a permanent tooth

Ha! You're just saying that so she'll put some money under your pillow.

You're my hero.

It will put roses in your cheeks.
It will make your face a healthy pink.

armed to the teeth
heavily armed

the tooth fairy
imaginary fairy who brings a gift when a child loses a tooth

to say something tongue-in-cheek
to say it jokingly

21

26

Home is where the heart is.
Family is the most important thing.

Look, Ma, our Virgil has finally come home, probably so he can attend the big hoedown on pages 34 and 35.

My Virgil!

Absence makes the heart grow fonder.
When someone is away, you love them more.

She is softhearted.
She is kind and sympathetic.

Cross my heart.

Can I keep it?

Cheer up, Clint. Things aren't so bad.

I didn't have the heart to tell him.
I was too upset to tell him the bad news.

Cross my heart.
I promise.

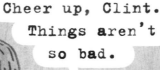

She had her heart set on it.
She wanted it very much.

Her heart was racing.
Her heart was beating quickly.

Here, grab this!

My heart sank.
I suddenly felt despair.

DANGeR: BewaRe of Quicksand

Can you find it in your heart to help?
Do you have the kindness to help?

I love a good rescue!

Big ♪ HoeDown TOMORROW NiGHT ♥ ♪ IN tHE HEART OF TOWN 7:00 'till MiDNiGHt

the heart of town
the central part of town

Fourscore and seven years ago ... Hello? I'm reciting a speech over here.

I learned it by heart.
I memorized it.

It does my heart good.
It cheers me up.

32

GET OFF MY BACK (BACK, SIDE)

Don't listen to him, Mr. Farmer. He's plenty fat enough to eat.

I want to get on his good side.
I want to make him like me.

Hi, Mr. Farmer, it's me, Terry; lovable, friendly Terry and way too skinny to eat.

OUCH!

He stabbed me in the back.
He harmed me when I didn't expect it.

Sorry, my bad.

All I said was, "If you were driving a tractor, you'd be a sheep at the wheel." It was a joke.

Baa, baad joke, Claude.

YIKES!

She's a thorn in my side.
She's a problem to me.

She turned her back on me.
She ignored me.

Nice job, dear.

Look, one-handed!

Give her a pat on the back.
Congratulate her.

I'm just massaging you with my teeth.

I'm afraid of cows!

What?

Bad kitty! Bad!!!

He has a yellow stripe down his back.
He is cowardly.

I could do it with one hand tied behind my back.
It would be easy for me to do.

backbiting
saying mean things

40

underfoot
in the way

Beat it!

Put 'em up
Put 'em up

Oh, I'm puttin'
'em up!

Tough toenails!
Too bad!
(sarcastic)

He was covered from head to toe.
He was completely covered.

Jim, I have some problems over here.

I have some brrrr . . . issues brrrr too!

I think we're on the wrong page. Has anyone seen a hoedown?

She took to her heels.
She ran away.

Don't step on any toes.
Don't offend anybody.

Lookie at us! We're space dancers!

feet of clay
a hidden weakness in a strong person

My feet are like ice.
My feet are very cold.

a real twinkle-toes
a good dancer

Put your best foot forward.
Make a good first impression.

Papa!

More pretzels?

to kick up your heels
to have lively fun

I followed in his footsteps.
I followed his example.

Stay on your toes.
Stay alert and ready for action.

Your drink, ma'am.

She was waited on hand and foot.
She was served with total devotion.

She has two left feet.
She's a terrible dancer.

We voted with our feet.
We left to show we were unhappy.

I second that!

Space monster! I vote we get out of here.

Pardon me.

Honk!

Oh no, pardon me.

The shoe is on the other foot.
The situation has reversed.

Left

Right

OtHeR

He shot himself in the foot.
He foolishly hurt his own chance for success.

foot traffic
the movement of pedestrians along a sidewalk

45

Index

For Dave—husband, best friend, inspiration, fun-maker—P. S.

**For Jessica and Hudson, thank you for making my heart sing,
melt, break and skip a beat on a daily basis—E. B.**

Text copyright © 2016 by Pat Street
Art and text balloons copyright © 2016 by Eric Brace
All Rights Reserved
HOLIDAY HOUSE is registered in the U.S. Patent and Trademark Office.
The art for this book was created digitally.
Printed and Bound in November 2015 at Toppan Leefung, DongGuan City, China.
First Edition
1 3 5 7 9 10 8 6 4 2
www.holidayhouse.com
Library of Congress cataloging-in-publication data
Street, Pat.
You're pulling my leg! : 400 human-body sayings from head to toe / by Pat Street ; illustrations by Eric Brace.
pages cm
ISBN 978-0-8234-2135-0 (hardcover)
1. English language—Terms and phrases—Juvenile literature. 2. Figures of speech—Juvenile literature.
3. Human body—Miscellanea—Juvenile literature.
I. Brace, Eric, illustrator. II. Title. III. Title: 400 human-body sayings from head to toe. IV. Title:
Four hundred human-body sayings from head to toe.
PE1689.S783 2016
428.1—dc23
2014037636

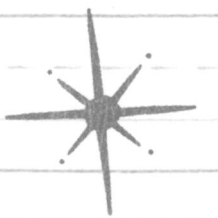
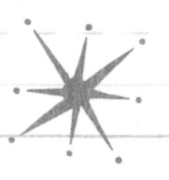